Let it Go
Let it Flow

21-Day Guided Journal to
Inner Peace through Forgiveness

Jaime Zazzara

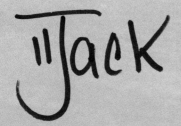

ISBN: 9781686339752
Imprint: Independently published

Introduction

Own Your Journey

Wherever you are right now in your life is exactly where you're meant to be. I'm so glad you made the decision to commit to the process of letting go and choosing forgiveness. You deserve to live in peace, no longer holding onto those low vibrational feelings such as guilt, shame, anger, resentment, jealousy, fear, worry, doubt, and self-sabotage. I know exactly what it feels like to keep attracting the same people and events into your life, wondering, "Why does this keep happening?" It's all related to the events and people you're subconsciously holding on to.

Are you ready to live a life filled with love, joy, abundance, and peace of mind?

Stop a moment and visualize what that looks like to you.
Close your eyes and imagine your "perfect life."
While nothing will ever be perfect, you can certainly come close to it.
Who are you with?
Where are you? What does it look like?
What are you doing in your ideal life?

How do you feel? I'm here to tell you that you absolutely deserve to and CAN live that life.

If you are willing to let go of what no longer serves you, you'll begin to attract all the things you desire.
Our lives are a direct reflection of our thoughts and feelings. What we think about ... we bring about. The law of attraction is simple, what you focus on you find. It doesn't differentiate from you saying YES, I want this or NO I don't want this - YOU attract it into your life. So why not think ALL the amazing things your life could be?

What if you met the love of your life and found your happily ever after? How about waking up every day genuinely happy and financially free to travel on your own terms?

Anything is possible based upon the decisions you make every day, especially if you surround yourself with like-minded people, free of drama and problems, focusing on joy and love.

This 21-Day Guided Journal allows you to release whatever is holding you back. All it takes is 15-20 minutes every day to complete the daily activities.

The intention is for you to choose forgiveness, release those feelings of guilt, shame, fear, anger, resentment, jealousy and learn to let go. Jaime Zazzara created *Freedom in Forgiveness Course* which gives you personalized coaching through this 21 Day Guided Journal. Find more information: https://jaimezazzara.com/freedom-in-forgiveness

Week 1: Self Awareness~ Release Guilt & Shame

Day 1: *Bridge the Gap* 💼

Affirmation: I am ready and open to change. I know it is a process and I surrender.

Activity: Where are you right now, and where do you want to be? See example:

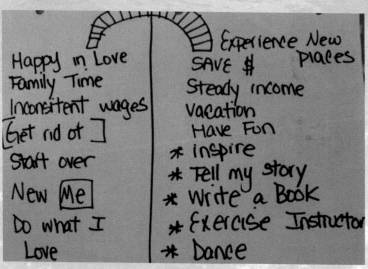

It may be easier to write out your thoughts and desires. Use this space to journal where you are right now, and where you desire to be. If you are unclear about what you want, how can you attract it into your life? Take some time to become clear on what your priorities are. Then you can take aligned action towards your goals.

_____

_____

_____

_____

_____

_____

_____

_____

_____

_____

_____

Where I am NOW	Where I want to be

Day 2: Who am I? 🧑‍🦱

Affirmation: I am aware of the thoughts and feelings I have about myself. I love myself for all that I am.

Activity: If you were to ask someone else to describe you, what words would they use? List those below:

_____

_____

_____

_____

Now, list the words that you feel describe yourself.

_____

_____

_____

_____

Creative Activity: I AM. Feel free to use a separate piece of paper to do this activity. See example

I AM

Day 3: *Truth vs Lies*

Affirmation: I love myself and know I was divinely created.

Activity: This is a powerful activity where you list all those inner beliefs about yourself that are holding you back from living your best life.

Fill out the Lie side first. Listen to the meditation: I am Light. Credit and rights to India.Arie - I Am Light (Lyric Video) https://www.youtube.com/watch?v=ism8dBjxKvc

Ask for guidance from your higher power and after you complete the meditation, complete the Truth side.

Example:

Truth	Lies
I am enough	I am not enough
I can be, do, and succeed at whatever I put my mind to	I can't be successful
I deserve to be loved unconditionally	I am not worthy of love

Truth	Lies

Day 4: *My core beliefs* ✳

Affirmation: I release all judgement, guilt, and shame ♡

Activity: Take a few minutes to think of how much you judge yourself in all areas of your life- health, relationships, career, money, parenting, self-image etc.

Write down 3 judgements you have about yourself (For example- I am not good enough. I don't deserve to be loved.)

1. _____

_____

_____

2. _____

_____

_____

3. _____

_____

_____

Change the statements to affirmations

I AM GOOD ENOUGH.

I DESERVE TO BE LOVED.

I Am ABUNDANT IN ALL AREAS OF MY LIFE

1. _____

_____

_____

2. _____

_____

_____

3. _____

_____

_____

If you choose, rewrite the first negative judgements on index cards and rip them up. Now, write the affirmations on sticky notes where you can see them. Repeat them to yourself when you find judgmental thoughts come into your mind.

Day 5: *Self-Acceptance* 👩

Affirmation: I accept that I did the best I could at the time with what I knew.

Activity: This statement was huge for me, especially through my divorce and the guilt I felt for my children. I blamed myself, feeling that I could have done more, or spared my children the emotional trauma they experienced. Guess what? I did the best I could at the time. This can be applied to so many areas of our lives.

Where do you feel blame? Towards you or someone else? It's time to forgive. Let it go and FREE yourself. Choose peace of mind.

_____

_____

_____

_____

_____

_____

_____

_____

_____

_____

_____

_____

_____

_____

_____

_____

_____

_____

_____

Day 6: *Letting Go* ✌️

Affirmation: I accept my past for what it is ... THE PAST. I am moving forward and choose to let go.

Activity: Letting go is a process. You must take it one day at a time, just like a recovering addict. Write your story and let it go.

_____

_____

_____

_____

_____

_____

_____

_____

_____

_____

_____

_____

_____

_____

_____

_____

_____

_____

_____

_____

_____

_____

_____

_____

_____

_____

_____

_____

_____

_____

_____

_____

_____

_____

_____

_____

_____

_____

_____

_____

_____

_____

_____

_____

_____

_____

_____

_____

_____

_____

_____

_____

_____

_____

_____

_____

Day 7: *My Triggers* 💣

Affirmation: I am aware of my triggers and choose to change my reaction.

Activity: Today, we will acknowledge our triggers and understand what causes us to react in a negative way. Most of the time, it's not about the person or event, but is a trigger that brings about past hurt. It is important to acknowledge these triggers that bring us back to those low vibrations of lack, fear, doubt, shame, and feelings of being unworthy. Then, we can replace them with love, understanding, compassion, and self-love.

List three things that cause you to get defensive, react, overanalyze, etc. My triggers are:

1. _____

_____

_____

_____

2. _____

_____

_____

3. _____

_____

_____

Week 1 Conclusion: My Happy Place Plan ☺

What are some things you can do to work through this when it occurs? It will happen! The point is to learn strategies to work through it. Ideas that work for me:

- Deep breath reset.

- Remove yourself from the situation (walk away and calm down).

- Be aware of the situations that will make you uncomfortable and avoid them.

- Listen to your happy music.

- Get outside and go for a walk. Moving your energy is huge. This is why dancing is such a release.

- Go to the beach and find your calm.

- Rapid appreciation ~ Call out or say in your mind all you are grateful for in that moment (your coffee, your car, the sun shining, etc.) It immediately shifts your vibration when you choose gratitude.

- Color or do something relaxing to you.

- Journaling is a great way to process and just allow yourself to release everything you're keeping inside. If this is not normal for you, it will take time to develop your practice.

- A morning pages ritual is so powerful, as it encourages you to wake up and put your stream of consciousness on paper. When I began practicing this, I experienced a huge shift in the connection with myself and my inner being. You are most connected to your higher power first thing in the morning when you wake up.

- Meditation is key to developing inner peace. No, I don't mean sitting crisscross applesauce and chanting OM. For me, meditation takes place in the a.m., and at night before bed using the 21-Day Guided Meditation with Oprah and Deepak. I use guided meditation allows me to listen to the words and retrain my mind. This is especially good when you have anxiety and the running reel of thoughts won't stop. Focusing on the words of someone else is helpful and allows you to find your calm.

What is your Happy Place Plan? Choose three things you will consciously do when you feel triggers coming on.

1. _____

_____

_____

_____

2. _____

_____

_____

_____

3. _____

_____

_____

_____

Week 2: Forgiveness

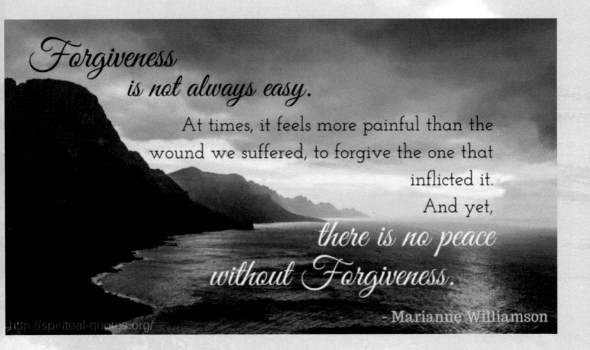

Day 8: *Forgive Yourself First* ✉

Affirmation: I forgive myself so I can have inner peace.

Activity: Write a letter to yourself forgiving whatever it is that you are holding onto. Let go of the guilt you hold towards yourself.

_____

_____

_____

_____

_____

_____

_____

_____

_____

_____

_____

_____

_____

_____

_____

_____

_____

_____

_____

_____

_____

_____

_____

_____

_____

Day 9: *Bless & Release Letters* 📑

Affirmation: I forgive those who have wronged me in order to live a life full of peace, love, and joy.

When you read this statement, who or what comes to mind as having wronged you in your life? Consider a person, or life-altering event that you would describe as having a long-term effect.

You may have held on to blame, anger, and resentment, but the only one suffering is YOU. No matter how bad it may have been, you deserve to live your life full of peace, love, and joy. Forgiveness
is about your peace of mind and accepting the wrongdoing as having nothing to do with you. Bless and release it.

Activity: Write a letter to each person you listed and discuss how you feel about the events and
have internalized them. You are not actually sending the letter, but the process of getting it out will be very therapeutic. You can do this with those who have passed as well.

Dear _____,

_____

_____

_____

_____

_____

_____

_____

_____

_____

_____

_____

_____

_____

With love and light,

Dear _____,

_____

_____

_____

_____

_____

_____

_____

_____

_____

_____

_____

_____

With love and light,

Dear _____,

_____

_____

_____

_____

_____

_____

_____

_____

_____

_____

_____

With love and light,

Day 10: *Forgiveness Ritual* 🦋

Affirmation: I surrender to my higher power to release my pain and suffering. I choose LOVE.
I forgive you *(name of person)* for *(how you were wronged)* even though it made me feel *(your painful feeling it caused)*.

I am ready to release any feelings of anger, guilt, shame, resentment, hate, or fear that I feel. Thank you for setting me free from the bondage of my bitterness towards (name). I now ask that you bless (name).

Return me to your light, filling my heart and soul with love for myself. Today I made a conscious choice to forgive and give my soul the peace of mind it deserves. May I continue to grow every day in love and light!

Activity: Practice this as many times as you need for each person you are forgiving.

Forgiveness Prayer

I SURRENDER TO MY HIGHER POWER
TO RELEASE MY PAIN AND SUFFERING
I CHOOSE LOVE

I FORGIVE YOU (NAME OF PERSON)
FOR (HOW YOU WERE WRONGED)
EVEN THOUGH IT MADE ME FEEL
(YOUR PAINFUL FEELING IT CAUSED)

I AM READY TO RELEASE ANY FEELINGS OF ANGER,
GUILT, SHAME, RESENTMENT, HATE, OR FEAR THAT I FEEL.

THANK YOU FOR SETTING ME FREE FROM THE
CHAINS OF BITTERNESS TOWARDS (NAME)
I NOW ASK THAT YOU BLESS (NAME)

RETURN ME TO YOUR LIGHT FILLING
MY HEART WITH LOVE FOR MYSELF.
TODAY I MAKE A CONSCIOUS CHOICE TO FORGIVE
AND GIVE MY SOUL THE PEACE OF MIND IT DESERVES.
MAY I CONTINUE TO GROW EVERYDAY
IN LOVE AND LIGHT!

JAIME ZAZZARA | WWW.BEHAPPYBEFREE.ORG

Day 11: *Grudges Be Gone* 🤲

Affirmation: My peace of mind and inner happiness is more important than holding a grudge.

I admit I am guilty of allowing petty things to cause anger and resentment towards friends and family. What realized is that #1, lack of communication may have caused why I felt wronged. If I had communicated my feelings, the outcome would have been different. I created an entire story in my head, none of which was true. # 2- Other people's actions are about them and when I take it personally, I am the one being affected.

Activity: Think of a relationship that may be strained and recall why. Reach out to this person and let it go. Holding a grudge is harboring negative energy. It is time to LET it GO and put your happiness first.
What grudges are you holding onto? Think big picture. If you lived everyday as if it were your last, who would you reach out to? Are you holding a grudge about something ridiculous?

_____

_____

_____

_____

_____

_____

_____

_____

_____

_____

_____

_____

_____

_____

_____

_____

Text or call this person and mend the relationship. Remember this is about YOUR inner peace. You are the one who suffers when you choose anger, resentment, jealousy, guilt, shame, etc.

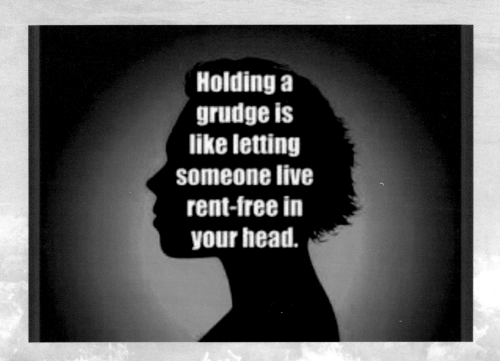

Day 12: *My peace of mind* 🙏

Affirmation: Today, I choose PEACE.

Activity: Draw whatever comes to mind inside the circle. This mirrors what is going on internally.

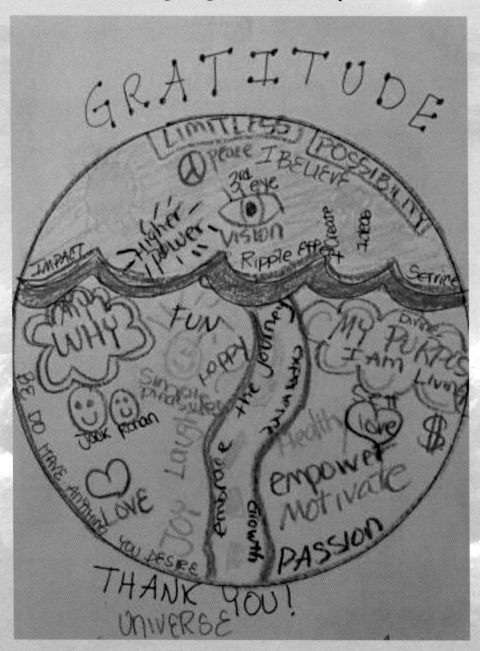

Day 13: *Set daily intentions* ☑

Affirmation: Old negative patterns no longer hold me back. I let them go with ease.

It is only natural for old patterns to surface as we grow into our best self. The idea is to develop awareness of your behavior and what triggers old habits. It also takes time to change a habit so be patient with yourself. Know that it is a decision to let go of the old you. Everyday wake up with an intention as to what you are working toward. It only works if you act every day. If you wish to be a better partner in your relationship, what are you doing daily to improve it?

Activity: Today, when you wake up, consciously set an intention for what you wish to accomplish, or your focus for the day. For example, if you want to feel more happiness or joy during your workday, what can you do differently to change your feelings?

Intention for today:

_____

_____

_____

_____

What I will do differently:

_____

_____

_____

_____

Intention for today:

_____

_____

_____

_____

What I will do differently:

_____

_____

_____

_____

Day 14: *Emotional Dumping* 🚚

Affirmation: I am aware of my emotions and allow myself to feel them

Activity: You have been working hard at letting go and releasing. Today I am going to ask you to take an emotional inventory of a typical day. List the emotion. When did it occur? What was happening? Why did you feel this way?

Emotion: _____

When: _____

_____

What: _____

_____

_____

Why? _____

_____

_____

_____

Emotion: _____

When: _____

_____

What: _____

_____

_____

Why? _____

_____

_____

_____

Emotion: _____

When: _____

_____

What: _____

_____

_____

Why? _____

_____

_____

Reflect: Is your behavior healthy or unhealthy?

Use this open space to do an emotional dump. What does that mean? Just write, write and write it ALL out. No blaming or reverting to a victim's mentality, just release any and everything on your mind. I find it best to do an emotional dump first thing in the morning.

_____

_____

_____

_____

_____

_____

_____

_____

_____

Week 3: ♡ Self-Love to Inner Peace 🙏

Day 15: *Self-love is priority number one* ♡

Affirmation: I am perfectly imperfect.

If you can't love yourself unconditionally, how can you love others completely? You were divinely created and perfect in every way. Accept yourself and stop the judgements towards yourself. You DESERVE LOVE.

Activity: Do something today for YOU! Practicing self-care is not selfish so let go of any guilt you may feel for taking time for yourself.

How do you show yourself love?

_____

_____

_____

_____

_____

Is it quiet time to read, going to the gym for a yoga class, getting together with a friend, getting a mani-pedi?

_____

_____

_____

_____

What is something you want to do for yourself?

_____

_____

_____

_____

Plan in the next two weeks when you will do this. NO cancelling or excuses. You deserve it!

Day 16: *Connect with your Inner Child*

Affirmation: I connect with my inner child and do things that bring me joy.

Activity: Today, I would like you to think back to when you were a child. What did you LOVE to do? Was it coloring? Riding your bike? Singing? Dancing? Swimming? Playing sports? Roller skating? Writing or drawing?

_____

_____

_____

_____

Things were so much simpler when we were children. We did the things we enjoyed that made you happy. Somewhere along the way as adults, we stopped having fun and laughing. It is time to reconnect with the little child within and have fun.

Today's activity is to be silly and do something you used to love as a child. Today, I will:

_____

_____

_____

How did you feel during or after?

_____

_____

_____

Take notice of how much you were living in the moment in pure joy and fun. It's time you bring that back into your daily routine. List all the things you enjoy and make it a priority to spend time having fun!

_____   _____   _____

_____   _____   _____

_____   _____   _____

_____   _____   _____

If you have children, it is great to do these things with them to have fun together. Even better ... include your partner if you have one. This exact reason is why relationships tend to drift apart because you lose the connection and fun.

Children are our greatest teachers as they have no fear, no doubt, and no worries. They live every day in the moment.

In the eyes of a child, you will see the *World...* as it should be.
~ Unknown ~

Day 17: *My Self-Care Plan* 🛁

Affirmation: I make myself a priority and practice self-care.

Journal Activity: I fill my cup first. When I do not practice self-care, I am out of alignment and all areas of my life fall out of balance. I know that self-care is not selfish.

- What is your self-care plan?
- Health, nutrition and exercise
- Drink water, eat healthy, move and exercise
- Quiet time alone: walk, read, take a bubble bath, color therapy, or journal
- Fun things that bring me joy: bike riding, walks on the water, jumping on a trampoline with your kids
- Spirituality/faith: prayer or meditation. How do you connect with your higher power?
- Personal development: read or listen to books
- Self-Care: manicure, pedicure, massage, facial, hair blow out, or buy yourself a new outfit

Nutrition Plan:

_____

_____

_____

_____

Exercise/ Fitness Plan

_____

_____

_____

Quiet/ Alone Time Plan

_____

_____

_____

Spirituality/ Faith Plan

_____

_____

_____

_____

FUN Plan

_____

_____

_____

_____

Personal Development Plan

_____

_____

_____

_____

Self-Care Plan

_____

_____

_____

_____

Day 18: *My Goals* 🗩

Affirmation: I believe in myself and can be, do, or have anything I desire.

Activity Goal setting: What do you desire? Jot down ideas:

Family/ Relationships	Health	Spiritual

Fun	Personal Development	Self-Care

My Goals: Family/Relationships

_____

_____

_____

Health & Wellness

_____

_____

Spiritual

_____

_____

_____

Career/Profession

_____

_____

Financial

_____

_____

Personal/Fun Goal

_____

_____

_____

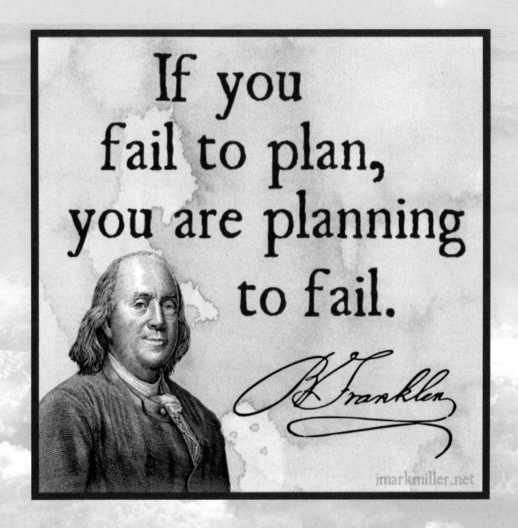

Day 19: *Prioritize and Plan* 📅

Affirmation: I am living my life in alignment with my goals.

Activity: It's one thing to set goals, and another to commit to the process and plan the action to achieve them. We all have the same amount of time in a day. It's up to us how we utilize our time. Do you need to get up earlier or stay up later? Do you need to delegate some of your responsibility so you can practice your self-care plan? Can you allow people to help you? Can you say NO to the things that are not on your priority list? Prioritize and schedule it in your planner.

I want to remind you to give yourself grace while working towards your goals. You will not be able to add in everything at once, completely overhauling your life. It takes time and consistency to change your habits. Be patient with yourself through the process.

Today's task is to organize your planner. I personally use an At-A-Glance planner and sync my events in my phone calendar. If I don't write it down, it doesn't happen. Here is an example of a color-coded calendar as an option. Each area of your life has a color (family, work, health, personal time, etc.)

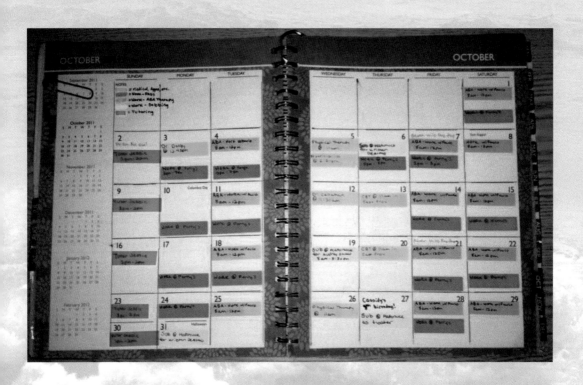

You can also use Google Calendar and use the same colors, so it is consistent. Happy Planning!

Day 20: *Live the Life you Dreamed* 🎉

Affirmation: I let go of all expectations. I am free to live the life I've dreamed.

Yesterday, you set goals and you are super excited about it. Life will get in the way of your goals and test you to see if you how serious you are.

It is possible you may not get the results you seek, as quickly as you would like. Do you give up? Do you stop and say it won't ever happen for you? Life happens and you lose your initial motivation.

Let go of the "should haves" and expectations. Commit and surrender to the process. Remember WHY you started in the first place. Be free to live your life the way you desire. This will take time and consistency. Develop your emotional endurance to stay the course, even when it feels like it's not working.

YOU'VE GOT THIS!

Activity: Today, write down why you set the goals you did. Imagine how you feel when you achieve those goals. Feel it and know that you absolutely can. Develop and attitude of, "Yes, I CAN!" You can choose to write yourself a letter a year in the future describing how you will feel when you achieve all your goals and are living your dream life.

To my future self,

_____

_____

_____

_____

_____

_____

_____

_____

_____

_____

_____

_____

_____

_____

_____

_____

_____

_____

_____

_____

_____

_____

_____

_____

_____

_____

_____

_____

_____

_____

_____

_____

_____

_____

_____

_____

_____

_____

_____

_____

_____

_____

Day 21: ♡ *Love surrounds me every day* ♡

Affirmation: I allow the energy of love and forgiveness to surround me.

On our final day of *Let it Go Let it Flow Challenge*, it is my wish for you to continue what we have practiced over the last 21 days. Surround yourself with the energy of love and forgiveness. You will be challenged by people and events that unexpectedly happen in your life. You have a choice of how you react and your attitude towards it. You could choose anger, blame, resentment or forgiveness, love, and inner peace.

Remind yourself every day: I choose my happiness, and I will not let anything outside of myself control me. I am creating a life that feels good on the inside and it will turn into experiences that are good on the outside.

Activity: Today's activity will be to listen to the Guided Meditation or podcast online here: https://anchor.fm/jaime-zazzara/

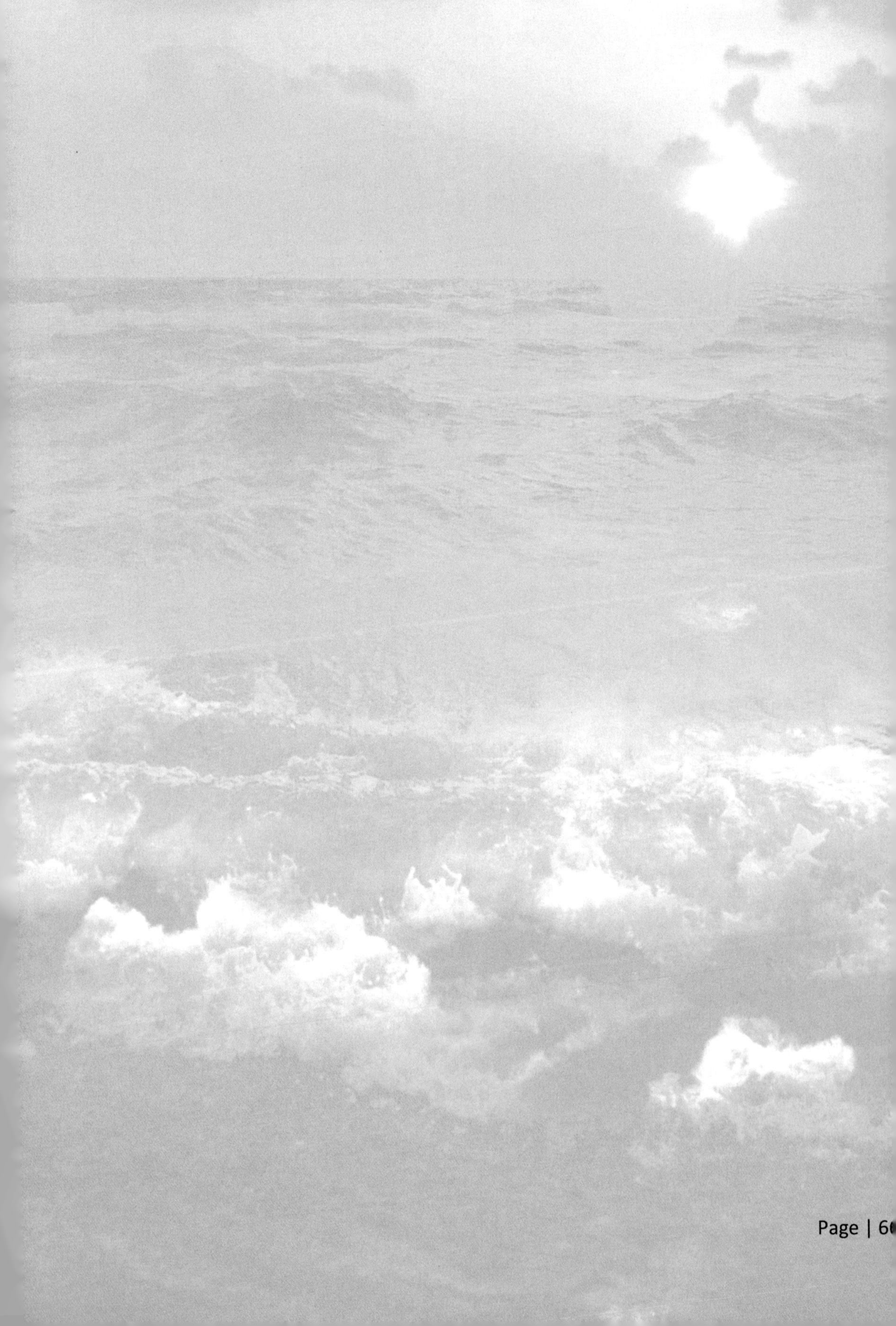

About the Author Jaime Zazzara has 19 years of experience as an educator, and teaching individuals of all ages is her natural gift. It has always been her mission to empower and instill a positive-growth mindset in everyone she meets. She found her purpose after experiencing a challenging divorce and healing after being co-dependent and married to an alcoholic. Born and raised at the Jersey Shore, she now resides in Ft. Lauderdale after she met her soulmate.

Jaime is a Professional Life Coach specializing in wellness, spirituality, and mindset. She assists women in letting go of the past while learning to love themselves while living a balanced, happy life. Jaime's goal is to spread love and light through empowerment, speaking, writing, and coaching while connecting and inspiring others.

Jaime offers services as a Spiritual Mindset Coach, Nutrition and Wellness Coaching, Motivational Speaker, Author, Online Courses and Sound Healing with Chakra Bowl Meditation. She hosts events: A Night of Forgiveness and Chakra Bowl Sound Healing Meditation.

Spiritual Mindset Coaching with Jaime

1:1 Spiritual Mindset Coaching

By embarking on a personal development journey and investing in a coach, you are saying YES to yourself! You will be able to discover your true authentic self. A spiritual journey is a very individual and intimate quest to consciously deepen your insight about you and your life's purpose. When we truly understand ourselves, we can step into our life's purpose. A spiritual journey can greatly help you to be more at peace with yourself and the world and can be a fantastic opportunity to let go of the past and stop worrying about the future.

By doing so, you may discover beneficial insights about the problems and challenges you're confronted with. Maybe you feel lost, overwhelmed, or unhappy and have that "stuck" feeling in your life. Spirituality Coaching is meant to be a guide for you to live a happy and fulfilled life.

1:1 Spiritual Mindset Coaching with *Jaime Zazzara*

🤍 Bridge where you are and where you want to be. What requires change?

🤍 Deciding your goal and create your vision for your life

🤍 Overcoming Obstacles-How do you anticipate obstacles

🤍 Changing your mindset to growth/positive mindset.

🤍 Raise your vibration- Joy, happiness, love instead of fear, doubt, anger.

🤍 Practicing self-care- Eating healthy, exercise, fun, meditation, yoga?

🤍 Surrender and let go of fear to the process- Believe in yourself. Don't compare where you are. Progress not perfect Focus on the what, not the how

🤍 Meditation Week- Be present and at peace

🤍 Bonus-Virtual Chakra Bowls Meditation Class

🤍 Forgive and Let go of the past. What is holding you back from living your best life.

🤍 Limiting Beliefs-Release drama and self- sabotage to live empowered

🤍 Organization-Scheduling-Time Management

🤍 Habits- Developing consistent routines and habits over time creates change

🤍 Reflect- Where are you in your journey to achieving your goals? Review goals and act

BE HAPPY BE FREE

PERSONALIZED CHAKRA HEALING MEDITATION

Personalized Chakra Healing Guided Meditation by JZ
https://jaimezazzara.com/personalized-meditation

The purpose of your Personalized Chakra- Aligned Guided Meditation is to retrain your thoughts and core beliefs by interrupting your current patterns of thinking. You will be guided with words specific to your goal. In addition, the Chakra Bowls will be played to clear your Chakras.

Personalized Chakra Healing Guided Meditation by JZ

Here are possible theme/focus for the meditation

❤ Self Love/ Self Image ❤ Self Worth/ Value (I am Enough)

❤ Forgiveness ❤ Letting Go ❤ Love/ relationships

❤ Releasing Fear ❤ Anger/Resentment ❤ Grief/ Healing

❤ Step into My Personal Power ❤ Procrastination

❤ Communication/ Use your Voice

❤ Creativity/ Being in the Flow ❤ Financial Abundance

❤ Health/ Nutrition ❤ Anxiety/Worry ❤ Depression

❤ Manifestation/ Law of Attraction

Recommended Practice: 21 Days listening to YOUR
Personalized Chakra-Healing Guided Meditation
In 3-5 business days, you will be emailed an audio recording via Google
Drive of YOUR Personalized Chakra-Healing Guided Meditation

Personalized Chakra Healing Guided Meditation by JZ
https://jaimezazzara.com/personalized-
meditation

Freedom in

Forgiveness Course

21-Day Challenge to Personal
Freedom through Forgiveness

HTTPS://JAIMEZAZZARA.COM/FREEDOM-IN-FORGIVENESS

Freedom in Forgiveness Course
with Jaime Zazzara

Week 1: Self Awareness~ Release Guilt & Shame
Day 1: Bridge the Gap 🌉
Day 2: Who am I? 🤔
Day 3: Truth vs Lies ☯
Day 4: My core beliefs ✳
Day 5: Self-Acceptance 🙏
Day 6: Letting Go ✌
Day 7: My Triggers 🎯
Week 1 Conclusion: My Happy Place Plan 🏖

Week 2: Forgiveness
Day 8: Forgive Yourself First 💛
Day 9: Bless & Release Letters 💌
Day 10: Forgiveness Ritual 🕯
Day 11: Grudges Be Gone 🚫
Day 12: My peace of mind 🧘
Day 13: Set daily intentions 📝
Day 14: Emotional Dumping 🗑

Week 3: ❤ Self-Love to Inner Peace 🕊
Day 15: Self-love is priority number one ❤
Day 16: Connect with your Inner Child🧒
Day 17: My Self-Care Plan 💆
Day 18: My Goals 🎯
Day 19: Prioritize and Plan 📋
Day 20: Live the Life you Dreamed 🌟
Day 21: ❤ Love surrounds me every day ❤

JZ
Jaime Zazzara

HTTPS://JAIMEZAZZARA.COM/FREEDOM-IN-FORGIVENESS

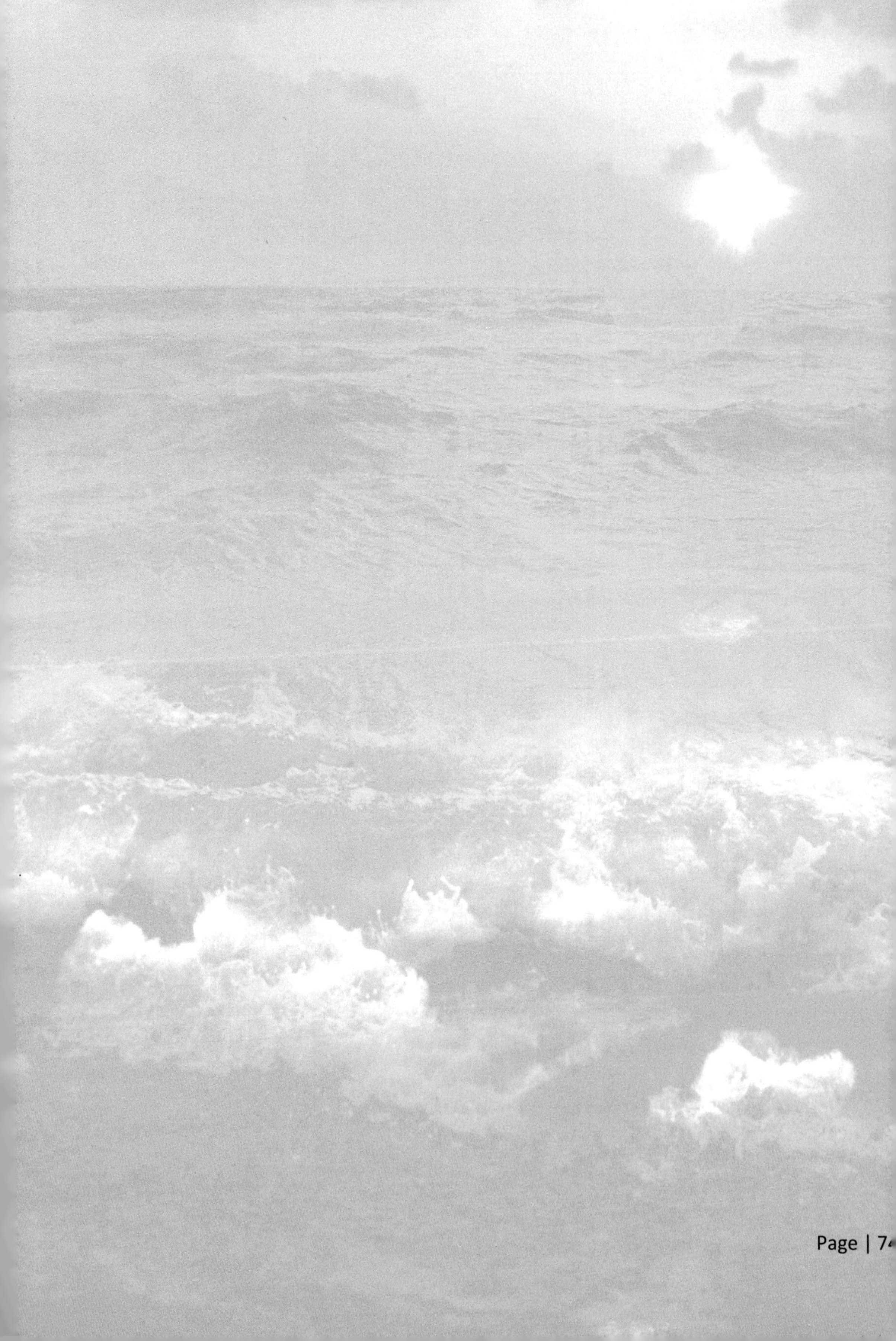

 FACEBOOK.COM/JZBEHAPPYBEFREE/

 INSTAGRAM.COM/JAIMEZAZZARA/

 HTTPS://TWITTER.COM/JAIMEZAZZARA

 HTTPS://WWW.LINKEDIN.COM/IN/JAIME-ZAZZARA/

 HTTPS://LINKTR.EE/JAIMEZAZZARA

 HTTPS://WWW.JAIMEZAZZARA.COM

 JAIMEZAZZARA@GMAIL.COM

Made in the USA
Columbia, SC
27 April 2020